Generalizations of a Banker

Arthur F. F. Snyder

Copyright © 2008 by Arthur Fenimore French Snyder

All rights reserved. No part of this book may be used or reproduced by any means, graphic, electronic, or mechanical, including photocopying, recording, or taping, or by any information storage retrieval system without the written permission of the author.

ISBN 1-4392-1547-2

Printed in the United States of America

Sculpture of the author by Kristin Lothrop

For Divinna-Jean Faust Snyder, who schooled with George Blanchine and for him danced Ballet Imperial, Rosalina, and Song of Norway; and for Agnes deMille, Oklahoma and Bloomer Girl, who abdicated a top Broadway career to raise, beautifully, three children, which permitted me to be a banker.

In Memoriam for Andrew

The leaves hang heavy in the trees
There is no wind to move the breeze
Our feet silently touch the ground
Our heavy hearts beat without a sound
A mother's love lives eternally
And can never be replaced
A father's pride rests spiritually
And both are God embraced

Judy's godfather
30 May 1995

Foreword

This collection of generalizations began in 1957 as notes for a speech. Ten ideas each began, "There is no such thing as..." and were used provocatively to excite the imagination of the listeners. New concepts were slipped into the "Speech File" over the years.

Often, associates criticize me for speaking in generalizations. Some can be quite condescending but I respond that generalizations are 80% true or they wouldn't be effective. My goal is not to be right but to stir the intellectual blood. I am never so happy as when a bright Harvard Business School student wipes me out. If I have made him think, I won.

Webster's Dictionary is on my side, however, for "to generalize" has no negative connotation. In fact, the definition fits my goal: "to derive or induce a general conception from particulars."

All knowledge consists of generalizations.
John Stuart Mill*

*Whenever quoted directly the name of the author is noted. If I have included another's idea without credit, it is without intent.

Arthur F. F. Snyder
Westwood, Massachusetts
August 8, 2008

Contents

Banking 13

Business 31

Finance 41

Lawyers 51

Management 59

Marketing 89

Nationalities 97

Philosophy 107

Religion 131

Women 147

Friends 157

Metamorphoses 199

BANKING

The Bank Charter

The banker operates under a special charter, which gives him the right to make money with other peoples' money. Because he is playing the game with the other guy's nickel, he needs both self-policing and government policing. Allowing plain companies to enter the competition amid government deregulation is to ignore history.

The Word of a Bank

The banker demands his customer be honest. Bankers should be certain to live by their word.

Speaking of a Bank

When the business leaders speak evil of a bank, their options cascade like a waterfall through their companies and out to the community. If they speak well of the bank, it flows gently as a summer stream through the meadow, which waters the fields and the stock, and "nurtures the farm."

THE MEASURE OF A BANK

Tradition compares banks by the amount of their deposits and the quality of the loan portfolio.

The true measure of a bank, however, is not the loans, but the character and ability of its depositors. A small, good depositor grows his business and the bank, but a big bad depositor brings calamity.

As Gresham said, "Bad money drives out the good."

THE GOOD BANK

The purpose of a bank is not to make money at the expense of its customers, but to prosper by enabling them to grow.

THE BORROWER'S INTENTIONS

When customers are trying to do the bank out if its money, there comes an instant, a very brief instant, when the bank must do the customer in.

THE GREAT DEPRESSION

The banks may not have caused the Depression but they sure made it bad by at least three activities, which any prudent banker should have foreseen.

1. Short-term mortgages. These had no long-term payout, so neither the owner nor the bank gained equity. When the bank needed liquidity, it called good loans as well as bad.
2. The banks loaned 90% of security values to anyone to gamble in the stock market. The market was climbing so steadily, the banker never bothered that sales clerks could not afford the interest. Not only did this drive the market way up, but when it turned, nothing could stop the margin calls on the way down.
3. The investment and commercial bankers were the same, so they gambled in the stock market with the depositor's money. The depositor had given it to the banker as a trust!

Without these three activities, the '30s might have been a recession instead of a depression.

Bankers

Good bankers make loans to strong companies. Weak bankers may loan to weak credits. Outstanding bankers support deserving people.

The Bank's Role

The bank's role in its community is to build businesses, not to destroy them. Some bankers are too quick to hammer a company into the ground before insisting on management corrections.

Relations With the Press

Of all institutions, banks should understand how to build a sound relationship with the press. Both the press and the credit department work in the same way. A bank builds a credit file for each customer. Over the years, each new officer reads the file and dredges up past discrepancies.

A newspaper builds a similar file, and a reporter in writing a story dredges up past problems.

With this similarity, a bank should tend its public relations files as carefully as a wise borrower.

THE CRIMINAL MIND

The good banker should be alert to the signs of the criminal mind. Some think criminals have specific traits:

1. Inveterate liars even when not necessary.
2. No respect for others' property. The fact that they want it is sufficient to make it belong to them.
3. They are optimists at all costs. Nobody will catch them.
4. They can be highly religious. Pray, steal, pray!

—*Dr. Stanton Samenow*

WHO IS RESPONSIBLE FOR NOT SPENDING THE MONEY?

Before lending or investing, be sure to identify the executive who is responsible for *not* spending the money. If you can't, don't play.

THE TROUBLED BANK

Never participate in a loan to a troubled bank no matter how good the loan is. When the troubled bank fails, it sells its bad loans to the FDIC and calls your good one just when it will hurt your customer the most.

BANKING A TROUBLED COMPANY

It may protect a company from bankruptcy to let the bank secure all the assets. The bank may overcome management's deficiencies in spite of the lawyer.

BANKING A CORPORATE FAMILY

Make loans to subsidiaries, not to the parent. Reality is in the "subs." Get the guarantee of the parent.

BORROWING FROM BANKS AND INSURANCE COMPANIES

Both banks and insurance companies misrepresent. The bank loans to you on a 90-day terms and renews it so often it becomes long-term debt. The insurance company lends long term with a 50-page document, which says that the debt is on demand if you fail to brush your teeth in the morning.

Both the bank and the insurance company can trap the unsophisticated borrower by these apparently opposite tactics.

Bank Heads

Particularly the chief executive officer of a bank should recognize that when a customer makes considerable complaint about a loan officer, the officer is usually right and has protected the bank's interests. Conversely, when a customer goes out of his way to praise a loan officer, the officer is usually wrong and has given away the bank.

The Tunnel Test

Loans should be made when light can be seen at the end of the tunnel—or at worst, the length of the tunnel is known.

Bonnie and Clyde

Bonnie and Clyde was not a movie about bank robbers; it was about banks. If we listened, we heard the audience cheer when they shot up the bank.

The Oakies and Arkies were good honest people, but God came and blew the soil away. The banks foreclosed and created *The Grapes of Wrath*.

If they had been rich institutions like the REITs of the '70s or the developing countries of the '80s, the ground rules would have been changed so the farmers could stay and work the farms. Shame!

The Banker's Hands

The banker holds the liquid assets of the people and businesses of his community in the palm of his hands. If he allows his hands to separate, not only must he blame himself, but the community must censure him.

Glass-Steagall

The Glass-Steagall Act of 1933 reformed the banking system, and under it we have had the most stable banking environment for 50 years. This is a record in the history of the country.

The erosion of the Act is unfortunate. One example is the resumption of the payment of interest on deposits. Banks paying interest require more and higher-interest loans to maintain profit. Managements inexorably stretch credit standards to predictable disaster.

WE AND THEY

In judging a loan officer in the bank, a dangerous negative telltale is how he identifies emotionally with the borrower. An early warning sign is that he uses the pronoun "we" in discussing the credit. Credit officers must understand the proper relationship: We is us, they is them.

A BANK SHOULD TRUST

Although many banks have "trust" in their name, too often they fail to live up to that quality. According to the *Encyclopedia Britannica*, two great British banks,

Lloyds and Barclays, were founded by English Quakers. Those banks prospered because they trusted.

Bankers' Greed

Every 20 or 30 years the bankers, by their greed, almost destroy the country. Witness the First Bank of the United States in 1795, the Second in 1813. Then 1860, 1890, 1929, 1973, loans to developing countries in 1990, and the sub-prime mess today.

Bankers in Business

Over the years I have seen many bankers leave to become treasurers or CFOs. Few have worked out. The sad fact is, the banker is used to discussing on Monday morning how someone else played the game on Saturday. Each banker deals with one hundred companies on an informal basis. He moves about in corporate society. He is not happy locked to one desk for ten hours a day.

Loan Demand vs. Rate

In the short term, loan demand varies directly with the rate. The higher the rate, the more demand for credit. As the rate falls off, demand for credit falls off. Traditional economics does not come into play for several months or even a year.

Banks and Commissions

Commissions and banking don't mix; when the banker lends money he has to get it back.

Banking Is Difficult

A moneylender loans to assets.
A banker loans to people.
Assets being hard are easy to appraise.
People being smooth are hard to assess.

Loan Committees

When discussing a loan, the loan committee members may become so involved appraising the assets they never get around to the credit discussion.

Unsecured Loans Are Safer

A credit should never have both secured and unsecured loans unless, of course, one is a long-term mortgage. Either the credit is sound as an unsecured loan, or it should be totally secured. If security is required for a loan, the whole credit should be secured. The unsecured loan is safer by definition!

SBA Loans

Besides the obvious problem that most SBA loans are weak to begin with, the structural problem exists that the SBA loan is a term pay-down lending against current assets, which can be dissipated rapidly without paying down the loan.

Daily Cash/Weekly Sales

Always watch the daily cash and the weekly sales.

Know vs. Think

A banker is interested in what you know more than what you think. When I ask, "What do you think?" it is really a challenging way of saying, "What do you know?" The banker then measures what you know against his own knowledge, from which he makes the decision.

REAL ESTATE DEVELOPERS

The morality of the real estate developer is not the same as a corporate borrower; the former exists as either a proprietor or a partner, with no laws preventing money from being transferred between entities. When he borrows against a piece of real estate, he considers that the bank is lending to the real estate—not to him. If the bank has to foreclose and it loses money on the asset, that was the bank's fault, not his. He rarely takes moral responsibility for the loan. In addition, income from his properties may be transferred at will, so long as he maintains the payments to the bank. Over the centuries, commercial banks have had more trouble from real estate than any other form of lending. Because of the mortality of the borrower, it will always be thus.

SIGNS OF TROUBLE

In the credit business, signs of trouble may be seen before the facts appear on the statement. Good credit officers see these signs the way the woodsman reads the forest and the sailor smells the sea.

The first sign of weakness is the deterioration of the cash position, which is followed by intermittent overdrafts, then by consistent overdrafts, and by the big overdraft over the long weekend. If things are really desperate, real knitting.

The reaction of the intermittent overdraft can be very revealing. If you begin to get, "Miss Jones was on vacation," or "It won't happen again," or "Gee, I have told her a dozen times," then it means money is getting tight. If the overdrafts are caused by checks on other banks, then it's time to run for cover. If they never apologize, these events can tell us months in advance there is "trouble in River City."

LEASING

A lease has four elements:
- Economics
- Credit
- Yield
- Tax

Of these, economics is by far the most important, for it determines security in the short run and the residual value, which is the real reason to be in the leasing business. Money can be lost on a triple-A credit if the economics aren't right. Economics is governed by "friction." If the leased equipment has friction (i.e., wear and tear), it will be maintained and will retain value. If friction is not present, as in a computer, final value is zero.

POWER IN VARIOUS COMMUNITIES

Money talks, but does it think?

LOANS

Sooner or later reality happens.

CROOKED RISKS

A bank cannot loan to a crook. Dishonesty is an inherent trait and very seldom overcome.

BUSINESS

Business Gambling

We hear people say that business is a gamble. They have used the wrong word. Business is a *risk*, but it is controllable by proper management. The course of the risk may be directed by the intelligence and judgment of the businessman.

Gambling is something else again. It is the stock market, the racetrack, and the football game. In those events we put our money down, but as soon as the window closes, our judgment no longer affects the events.

Profit Is Not!

Profit is not the reason a company is in business. There is only one reason for a company to be in business: to gain a customer and to keep that customer. Profit is the necessity for staying in business.

A Company Is a Four-Legged Table

All companies, big and small, have four legs: research, production, marketing, and finance. If the table is to stand level, these legs must be of equal importance.

BOARD OF DIRECTORS

The board has one job: to elect the CEO, and then support him. The hard part is saying "goodbye" soon enough.

CORPORATE PURPOSE

The purpose of going into business is not to make money. We go into business to do something worthwhile. If we do that right, we make money.

General Motors thought they were in the business of making money and forgot about making automobiles. Of the ten major improvements of automobiles in recent years, not one came out of Detroit, which was busy making money. Or were they?

THE NATIONAL PASTIME

The national pastime is not baseball or football or television; it is business.

Fortunately for America, anyone can go in business and engage in that pastime. Win, lose or draw. It is this opportunity that provides the challenge and the glory and the hope of America.

Corporate Buildings

When the chief executive builds a corporate headquarters, sell the stock.

The New Significant Shareholder

Don't ignore him. Put him on the board of directors. He then becomes part of the problem, and he should help to solve it.

Originators

The saddest words of tongue or pen are not Whittier's "It might have been," but the limitations of originators. Technological originators in particular create companies because of their genius, because they psychologically do not fit into large organizations. If they are successful in their own company, eventually they have a big company and they, themselves, do not fit into that big organization, although it is their own. Sometimes they have to be pushed out of the management. Sadly, they never go quietly, and they never really understand.

No President

Big companies have chairmen, presidents, treasurers, controllers and secondary titles of CEO, COO and CFO.

Small companies should not rush to big titles. Really, they do not even need to have a president. The new little company has a manager, a foreman, an engineer, a clerk. But most important: a salesman.

Some Buy, Few Build

Financial entrepreneurs buy businesses, but seldom build businesses. They may manage them so the business grows, but the actual building of a company starts with men of ideas. Such men are rare indeed.

If not a man of ideas, the next best thing is to be able to recognize such men and to support them.

Fledgling Companies

If the president of a brand new company sets his own salary above his pay at the big organization he just left, the company is doomed to failure. If he increases his salary, everything he does is increased in cost—the rugs on the floor, the size of his office—everything will be more expensive.

On the other hand, if he sets his own salary lower, everything he does will be controlled, and his new company will profit and prosper.

To Start an Enterprise

10 men are too many

3 men are plenty

2 men are sufficient

1 man is best

The Thought Leader

Particularly, the head of a technological company must be its thought leader. He must more than understand the technology—he must have a vision of the technology.

Innovation and the Engineer

The engineer is captive to his learned knowledge. But, the inventor applies untrammeled, intuitive knowledge to his environment, which leads to a new idea. Eventually the engineer is asked to put the idea to work.

Entrepreneurs

The successful entrepreneur needs four things: ego, timing, uniqueness, and hunger.

Problem Situations

Stop going backward before you can go forward.

Troubled Companies

They need either a third party to sell them, or a first party to run them. Of course, the first should be first.

THE BUGGY WHIP

In declining technologies, the lone surviving company may be a big winner.

BUSINESS HYPOCRISY

The corporation is a hypocrite. The corporate executive blames the government if business isn't going well, but he wants the government to stay out of his business.

He predictably pollutes Los Angeles, but hates regulation. He misleads the stockholder, but gets mad at the SEC. The list is too long.

The corporate executive hires a man at 23 and says, "Be Loyal," but if the guy gets a little tired at 50, he cans him.

The corporate executive hates communism, but certainly runs a fascist structure.

TABLE, BRIBE, AND GIRL

There are the fundamentals of an acquisition.

Generalizations of a Banker

The stated reason a company can be purchased is on top of the table. The real reason is underneath and must be ferreted out perhaps by speaking to former employees.

In every acquisition, someone can make it difficult, not necessarily the major shareholder. Seek that person out and satisfy his needs. The "bribe" may be as easy as staying in the corner office.

When big-city company is chasing small-country company, the little guy is just as smart but insecure. Don't try to impress him. When wooing a girl, don't tell her how handsome you are—convince her how pretty she is. When she believes that you think she is the most beautiful girl in the world, it is amazing how handsome she thinks you are.

FINANCE

The Financial Man

He should ask "Yes, but" questions.

The Controller

He is like a rolling mill, which squeezes the hot ingot into shape. Sparks fly as the white-hot steel is tortured by the hard rolls. He doesn't make the steel or cut it or fabricate it, but he shapes it and controls it.

Finance

Sooner or later, companies are *managed* by people who are *financially* oriented.

The New Treasurer

The person to be treasurer is one who is such because he *was* such. It should not be an untrained investor, and the statistical chance that he happens to be your brother-in-law is too low even to discuss.

Scorekeeper Should Stay Out of the Game

The CFO (controller/treasurer/chief financial officer) should not have line or operating functions. It is his duty to identify the problem and to keep score. If identified with operation problems of his own, he can't score his peers. The umpire can't also play first base.

Why Are You Funding?

If it's to cover equipment, bricks and mortar, and long-term debt, it is suitable. If it's to cover working capital, or some short-term debt, it is suitable. If it's to cover marketing and research, it better be equity.

Corporate Figures

There are only two figures in a corporation that really count: sales and profits. If these are what they should be, all others will follow in line. The corollary is that sales and profits won't occur if the others are out of line.

Accounting

Both internal and external accountants have a duty to practice the "looking forward" aspect of their profession. This function requires discipline and judgment.

Accountants

The problem with accounting is the accountants are telling the managers what information they need to manage, and the managers no longer have the option of telling the accountants what they need to manage.

Bad Audits

The most damaging audits on the national scale have not been on bad companies, but on those that appeared to be twice as good as their competition. As examples: Equity Funding, Viatron, National Student Marketing, Bank of the Commonwealth. In each case, these companies put out reports that showed them doing at least twice as well as their competition. There are just too many telephones in the world for any one company to be any order of magnitude better than its competition.

If partners in the Big Seven* firms, while shaving in the morning of the day they are to sign the audits of companies that are ostensibly twice as profitable as all competition, would only put down their razors and say, "There is no such thing. I won't sign 'till I find out what's wrong," how much better off the accounting profession would be, not to mention the investors.

*The Big Seven accounting firms don't exist anymore because of this very problem.

Timelines of Reports

Figures late indicate loss. Figures early indicate profit.

Long-Term Loans

The covenants of long-term loans are always violated! Therefore, before you sign the agreement, be sure you can live with it and that the bank will be understanding should minor problems occur.

Of course, major insurance companies will live with the terms of the loan. Be doubly certain that you understand the impact.

Public Debt

When a company plans public debt, that debt will "look under the rug." Debt supplied by banks is more casual and short-term. It looks to short-run assets in case of trouble. Long-term debt will look under the rug and tie the company up in tighter knots. This discipline can be good for the company, although possibly embarrassing.

Cash Flow Is a Booby Trap

Every decade or so, there is a new financial fad. For a while it was liability management, then it was cash flow.

Cash flow comes from two sources: first, depreciation, which anticipates refurbishing of plant. When that time comes, at least twice the amount of depreciation will be necessary to rebuild the plant, so appropriate funds with care.

The second source is after-tax profit, which is the only cash flow. So profit is important, and nothing else counts. Don't search for cash flow. Seek profit.

Real Estate Investment Trusts—The Five Wrongs

1. *Wrong* to go public from scratch. The REITs went public from the starting gate. They should have had private placements and operated for several years to get a real track record.
2. *Wrong* to invest immediately. The REITs had to invest 90% from the very beginning, which forced them to make bad loans immediately.
3. *Wrong* to pay out 90% income. The REITs were forced to pay out all the income they had as dividends so that no surplus was built up as a cushion.
4. *Wrong* not to have real reserves. Because the REITs were instantly public, they could not afford to penalize the earnings by proper reserves.

5. *Really wrong* to have false accounting. In entirely too many instances, loans were made to customers of the REIT on which interest was not to be paid until the end of the term of the loan. Interest was added to the note or incorporated in the original borrowing. Therefore, the REIT not only had no real cash income, but was paying out dividends on no cash income. The age-old problems of accounting theory destroy the REITs. There is no such thing as income unless you can pay the help with it on Friday.

Computers Are Simple

A computer can do only two things: it can add one and one (one may be negative), and it can remember that it did. Its uniqueness lies in its ability to do so many additions and so very fast. All of its logic is man-made.

Stock Issues

Early stock issues are sold to the public on expectations. Later, stock issues are based on reality.

Fad Investments of the Day

Before investing in fancy investment gimmicks such as tax shelters and the darling of the moment, consider that sound men do not contribute their lives to the operation of such endeavors.

Acquisitions

The best acquisitions I have seen came from buying divisions from mammoth companies. Major corporations, because of good accounting, squeeze the assets and the profits and overburden themselves with overhead. With minimal profits, sooner or later corporate management decides to divest. The price is always realistic (for there are no stockholders), price-earning ratios, or incumbency egos in the way. The price, if book, is fair and nearly always acceptable by the corporation board.

Accountants as Salesmen

Were accountants salesmen, they would not refer to their best opinions as "unqualified," which has a negative connotation.

LAWYERS

Justice

When introduced to a lawyer of significance, I ask, "Who is responsible for justice?" The answers are tragic, even from judges and prosecutors. The answer is the Constitution: We the people of the United States, in order to form a more perfect union, *establish justice!*

Legal Veracity

Many lawyers lie. Criminal lawyers are superior at it!

Legal Trust

Never put all your trust in a lawyer. Particularly your own!

Esquire

Americans consider the appendage "Esq." affected, though widely used in Britain by gentleman and professionals. In the United States, the lawyers cling to Esquire as a special right and title. Since the law may no longer be a profession in this country, but a greedy business, perhaps we should abandon that title in addressing our lawyers.

Lawyers and Business

It has been said that war is too important to be left to the generals to decide. Business is too important for the lawyers to decide.

Legal Fees

Lawyers may quote hourly rates, but fees rarely reflect hours. If you are doing something worthwhile, the fees follow a percentage of the transaction. If you are in trouble, fees represent a percentage of the money available. If you have done something really bad, the fee approaches your net worth.

Adversary

Lawyers are schooled in an adversarial relationship. If they enter business, often they work against—and not with—their associates.

Congress

Should it be against the law for a lawyer to be in Congress? Or in a state legislature?

Law Suits

Ninety percent of the people who sue should be sued.

Legal

Corporations with public shareholders now have audit committees comprised of outside board members. The board can then select auditors independently of the management. Since lawyers represent the management that hires them, rather than the board of directors as a whole—or more importantly, the shareholders as a group—it's time to have a legal committee of outside directors. Then the lawyers will know to whom they report.

The 50/50 Rule

A lawyer is fortunate if he knows 50% of his client's problem when he takes the case. A client is fortunate if he knows 50% of his lawyer's problem when the lawyer returns from court. With such lack of candor, is there any wonder that mistrust exists?

Lawyers

We can identify two types of lawyers, shyster and non-shyster. Although difficult for them to sort out which is which, we really never can be sure.

Great

Problems make money for lawyers, and we pay the bill. If they lose, they still make money, but we sell our homes to pay.

Right and Wrong

Attorneys are not concerned with right and wrong. A good attorney is concerned with what the law says about what his client did, or what the law would say about what his client wants to do. Bad attorneys are concerned with how to get around that law.

Rates

When we hire a lawyer at an exorbitant hourly rate, he never comes alone, which, at best, doubles the rate.

Tort

Man has known for millennia that it snows every winter and snow is slippery. If someone slips on new snow on my sidewalk, how can some tort lawyer advertise that I should be sued? What a greedy, destructive bunch!

Lobbyists

If you want to know what is in the heart and mind of an industry, find what its lobbyist is up to. Its P.R. department may be on the other tack.

THE ULTIMATE QUESTION

Watergate created the ultimate question on politics: Is it illegal for non-lawyers to be dishonest in politics? Stated another way: As a non-lawyer, how did Haldeman get in the club?

HISTORY'S TWO BIG MISTAKES

Moses' lawyer did not get the Palestinian's god to sign the deed to Canaan. Moses' geologist did not give good advice on what land to accept from God—no oil!

COMPANY COUNSEL

Bad management may be supported by the company's counsel. Sometimes it is necessary to alert that counsel to the problem he is abetting.

CRIMINAL LAWYER

The term criminal lawyer is a sequitur.

Management

Corporate Attorney

There is no such thing as a corporate attorney. Management hires the attorney and he does its bidding for better or for worse. If management is good, counsel may be good. If management is bad, the attorney supports incompetence no matter how able he is. In either case, good or bad, the shareholders, the directors, the employees, the customers, and the suppliers are not represented by corporate counsel. Any lawyer who thinks otherwise will be replaced by management.

Profit Before Taxes

There is no such thing as profit before taxes. Uncle Sam is going to take half of it no matter what. Talking about profit as though you own it before you have paid the taxes is unreal and misleading to your thinking. Therefore, always talk about profit after taxes.

Arson

No insurance company has ever paid a claim and never will! The policyholder pays the claims after paying for tall buildings. If the insurance company really paid the claims, it would do something about arson, body shops, and tort lawyers.

Lack of Capital

There is no such thing as lack of capital, only lack of management—because if you have good management, capital will beat down your door trying to invest.

Control

There is no such thing as control, only good management. If you control 100% of a company and have poor management, the trustee in bankruptcy will control it for you.

Underhead

There is no such thing as overhead. It's really *under*head. That is, the costs of management are created by the heads of the bosses, not by the heads of the workers.

Corporate Income Taxes

No corporation has ever paid income taxes, and none ever will. The corporation passes its taxes along to the consumer, who pays them every time he buys a toothbrush or a gallon of gasoline. Politicians pretend to be taxing business and seek credit for saving the people taxes. Actually, the politician reaps enormous sums when the government spends, which, if the people really understood, they would put the politician out of work and cut down the political bureaucracy. Corporate income taxes rob the poor and give to the rich, for the rich can afford the hidden taxes on necessities.

Profit Before R&D

There is no such thing as profit before R&D. If R&D is not included as a selling expense, any company will wither and die. Every 5 or 10 years every company is rejuvenated with new, updated, modern products, whether it be dresses or cars or technology. If the R&D is not expensed, profit is overstated and the investors deluded.

Sound Management Principles

There is no such thing as sound management principles. Managers do not talk about sound management principles; they talk about what they are going to do, and their plans become sound.

Selling Stock

No company in the history of the world has ever sold stock. That is not what happens. Stock is not the commodity; money is the commodity. The company buys capital and pays for it with stock. Stock is the vehicle for payment. You do not pay with a number of shares, you pay in a percentage of the company.

Four Kinds of Money

The entrepreneur should understand the liability side of his balance sheet. Cash is an asset on the left side. Money in the financial sense is on the right. There are four kinds of money:

1. The kind you rent
2. The kind you lease

3. The kind you buy
4. The kind you earn

By example, the treasurer *rents* money from the bank but *leases* with a long-term mortgage. He *buys* capital and pays for it with stock. Money is *earned* and increases the equity. Finally, the fifth is *paid* in dividends.

THE FORMER BOSS

Few previous employers tell the truth. If the prospective employee was outstanding, his employer considers him disloyal for leaving. If the prospective employee was bad, the employer does not want to prevent him from getting the job. Either way, skilled interviewers can get fooled by the former boss.

BOTH JOBS

Every man has two jobs—the one that needs to be done and the one he wants to do.

Problems

Good men, when they go to bed at night, think about their problems. When they get up in the morning, they think about their problems. If men talk about how good things are and never speak to the problem, they are unaware or lying.

Management Is Not Friendship

If we personally like a bad manager, perhaps we should say goodbye. If we personally dislike a good manager, we can never say goodbye.

Look at the Secretaries

On visiting a company, always look at the secretaries. The secretary represents the executive. Within a few seconds you learn what his values are, whether he is busy, whether he expects performance or glamour or both. Most important of all, she reflects his sense of courtesy and respect for visitors and associates.

Charity

When a chief executive officer is absorbed in fund raising, the company suffers. Either be sure someone is watching, or get someone else to raise money.

Task vs. Goal

Corporations are either task or goal oriented. When task, subordinates are told how to do their functions according to strict rules. Don't think, just do. When goal, associates are included in the planning, are provided with the tools, and are free to perform to their ability.

Be an Executive

No matter what your title, you are not an executive unless your secretary always knows where you are and how to reach you.

Troubled Companies

Troubled companies have only one problem: the guy in the corner office!

Survival

In all my years I've never seen a troubled company survive unless someone has come with the courage to cut the company back so that it is profitable.

Board Meetings

Excessive time is devoted to management prerogatives, salaries, options, promotions, titles, insurance, and very little to the business.

Leased, Not Owned

Companies do not own their employees. We merely lease their brains and manpower.

Corporate Objective

Money may be the final reward but it is not the objective. The objective is to build something of value.

Corporate Value

Marx was right: only productive labor adds value at the gross margin level. But if not productive enough, no one wins.

Profit and Loss

Between a dollar of profit and a dollar of loss, there is much more than a two-dollar difference.

What Assets?

The one thing bad management can do well is to dissipate the assets of a company right before your very eyes.

Executive Overpayment

Most of our major corporations overpay their chief executive by startling amounts. This, in spite of the evidence that these organizations are losing business abroad. Worse, in the car industry these guys are importing Japanese managers to teach them what they are overpaid to know.

Management Reinforcement

Executives and managers usually reinforce their associates or subordinates either positively or negatively. If negative, fear, lack of confidence, and sullenness are used. No matter how good the result it's never quite satisfactory. If positive, praise, encouragement, and grace are used. If a problem occurs, help and support are given. Strangely, the one who manages by negative reinforcement often pays more than the positive reinforcer.

Overpaid Presidents

Overpaying the president of a small- or medium-sized company has one of two results. Either all the salaries are too high, or only the president gets the gravy and good associates can't be hired. If the president is fairly rewarded, the company has a better chance for salary balance.

Aircraft

Aircraft in a small business is the first sign of failure.

Corporate Assets

The real assets of a company walk out the door every night and back in the next morning. If the owners don't understand this, they will make fatal mistakes.

A Sense of Urgency

Among other qualities, a leader transmits a sense of urgency.

QUALITY LEADERSHIP

Don't buy principal equipment or services from organizations with a bad leader.

CONSULTANTS

Consultants come in two styles. Best, the well-educated, brilliant, aggressive report writers. Second best, the recently unemployed executive. Both work for management and seek to please. Even so, they may be brilliant and very effective. But be wary of hiring consultants as executives in your company. They are bright but have little management experience or were let go because they didn't.

THINKERS: FACTUAL VS. CONCEPTUAL

Factual thinkers are foreman, managers, and administrators. Conceptual thinkers are leaders.

BUILDING A COMPANY

Some very bright men lack dexterity so they keep knocking down building blocks. Sadly, their conceit causes then to knock down the able man's blocks, too.

Courteous Employees

Why am I surprised when managers complain that their employees are not courteous? If you treat people with respect, you will have respectful people. If you treat them as peons, you get peons.

Shareholders

Every additional shareholder is another problem. Big shareholders can be big problems and lots of little shareholders can be a big problem. When making corporate decisions, sit back and think of yourself as the smallest shareholder, then act.

Patience

There are two kinds of patience: active and passive. Passive patience is when one person permits another to act as he will, without restriction. Active patience is when a manager, knowingly, but helpfully, watches another's performance.

THE NEED TO DIVERSIFY

So many companies have diversification as a goal, but diversification usually brings failure, not success. Management brings success.

THE INCUMBENCY COST OF PEOPLE

It's traditional to think that good, bright, young people are promoted around and over inferior incumbents. That is not what happens. Good people do not wait to be promoted around an inferior; they quietly leave, which is a terrible incumbency cost for the company, for the inferior stays on. And the cycle continues.

THE BEST ONES

It used to bother me that the best ones would stay a few years and then leave to do better things.

Today, those are the people who provide me the most pride and the most satisfaction.

Juniors and Seniors

We do not have subordinates who work for us. We really work for them, and particularly, for the juniors. We should provide every asset to enable them to be effective: the tools, the time, the encouragement, the patience, and the rewards.

Greener Pastures

When you are unhappy in your job and seek another, remember that you will take yourself with you and likely find the same problem to vex you.

Janus Has Three Heads

People have three relationships in business: the way they act with the people above them, alongside them, and below them. Occasional friction with peers is normal if it results from sincere dedication to the job. It's not so destructive as long as it arises from honest conviction. Superiors can be bluffed for a surprising length of time. Subordinates can be bluffed up to a year. After that, never.

Corporate Manners

Some spread oil on troubled waters, but others add that oil to the smoldering fire of human relationships.

Eugene Fubini

Long-range planning is so you'll know what not to do when the time comes.
— *Director of Long-Range Planning, IBM Corporation*

Success

The gift of giving associates more credit than they deserve.

Hiring Allegiance is Forever

Just as a woman always remembers her first lover, we always have a fond allegiance to the person who hires us. It is a true compliment, for it says our talents have value.

Delegation

The managers who wish do so everything themselves and delegate with difficulty are often the ones who insist that their superior delegate without reservation. They complain that they must do the work if it is to be done right but resent the boss following up on their work.

Management

In judging a manager, we must ask, "Does he see the people he is looking at?"

P&T Disease

Small companies, through the ego of the founder, often have P&T disease: the president and the treasurer are the same person.

The functions of these two jobs do not rest easily in the mind of one person. It is the president's responsibility to build the company and manage the assets to their optimum. It is the treasurer's responsibility to provide the cash and the financing for the venture. One says, "Let's Go!" The other says, "Yes, But!" They are a team that needs to listen to each other and neither can be always right.

Fire Fighters

Some managers fight fires continuously. No matter how extraordinary, a manager can only fight four fires at once. He can have a hose in his left hand, pointing one way, and a hose in the right hand, pointing another way; he can spit on one; and pretend he is a small boy at his first campfire for the fourth. The rest will just have to keep burning.

Manpower Expense

If management wastes money on assets, at least they can be sold at some price. When it wastes money on extra manpower, that expense is gone forever. You never get the salaries back.

Executive Authority

Once an executive abdicates his authority, he can never regain it.

Former Friends

Hiring friends does not build a business and it sure destroys friendships.

Friendship

The executive should be friendly with his associates; he may be a "friend in need," but never a family friend.

Cooperation

A company needs people who work at the job, not *at* each other.

Hiring People

There are four fundamentals:
1. Intensity
2. Capacity

3. Character
4. Grace

References

When hiring a new employee, always check someone who has worked *for* him. We can fool superiors, but our associates know all about us.

Hiring

Can he do what he should do? Will he do what he says he can do?

Four Jobs

Each job is really four jobs:
1. What the boss thinks the job should be.
2. What the incumbent thinks the job should be.
3. What is being done.
4. What really should be done.

ORGANIZATION IS NOT BOXES

Companies are not a bunch of boxes piled up on an organization chart. They are really departmental pyramids with an individual at the top of each. The size if that pyramid or its slope depends upon the individual at the top and how he manages. Each pyramid has a proper slope, narrow or wide, depending upon the numbers of people that should be within it to accomplish the function. Neat boxes do not dramatize the pyramidal relationship.

LIABILITY MANAGEMENT

Liability management is not real; it is a misleading phrase. It should not imply overall management. What is really meant is management control or structure of the liabilities. We manage assets, which are real, and the earnings from those assets serve the liabilities. Liabilities did not exist until a few hundred years ago, for double-entry bookkeeping came into being at that time. People have been in business for 10,000 years without liability management.

THE GAME PLAYER

The executive game player thinks he covers up his arbitrary decisions by such ploys as "fix up that office for good old George," when in fact he has already hired an outsider but doesn't want to reveal the new move yet. The game player thinks he is smart, but the organization learns of the new executive from other sources, and he is humiliated by the cover up. Actual corporate harm occurs when a real plan is taken to be another game!

PROMOTIONS

A good boss doesn't promote you, your peers do. If your peers do not accept your promotion, the boss can't accomplish it. If the boss is foolish enough not to understand that, sooner or later the frustrated peers will get you.

DIVERSIONS

We must identify the opportunity cost of diversions, which deter companies from progress. The examples are obvious: travel, golf, wet lunches, etc. The cost of those diversions can add up to failure.

Company Politics

All companies are political, for each of us is. Therefore, we cannot set a goal of no politics in the company; we can only, and we should, set a goal of loyalty and respect for each other.

A Communications Stockade

A company is a big square with the chief executive at its center. In each corner is the bank, its shareholders, its customers, and its employees. There is a line of communication between the chief executive and each corner. If the banker finds a barrier in the communication, he will find it in the other three corners as well, and the chief executive has surrounded himself with a communications stockade. Sooner or later, the company will implode around him.

Moving

Moving companies is the road to bankruptcy. It costs money to teach the janitor where the new broom closet is. And from there up, it's just one massive problem.

The Corporate Rally

Strong corporate managers must learn the art of rallying with each other. The greatest professional tennis players organize a rally with a friend to improve their game. While doing it, they do not try to score points. It takes two to rally, and, if each player's game is to improve, one must not try to kill the rally with a sudden smash.

The same is true in business. Managers must be able to sit down with each other and rally their ideas back and forth without one winning a devastating point.

Consultants

Permanent consultants indicate basic management weakness and lack of leadership.

Hearing and Seeing

The test of a manager is knowing what he is not hearing and seeing what he is looking at.

Psychological Travel

If the senior officer responsible for an organization is continuously traveling on "important" missions, something is wrong with the company, or will be. Travel is an escape from the reality of the job, which begins at your desk at eight o'clock every day and may not end when you go home at night.

Corporate Receipts
or His Finger on His Number

Each officer in the Navy has a signal number by which he is identified. The naval career depends upon keeping black marks off that signal number, so a lesser officer spends most of his time "keeping his finger on his number" so that it will not become besmirched.

The corollary in the corporation is the "corporate receipt." These are found in the form of many memoranda written in all directions as a record of what the writer did, or did not, have responsibility for whatever did, or did not, happen. The confident and sound manager is perfectly content with word of mouth and the telephone. He does not need "corporate receipts."

Measuring Managers

A manager, unwilling to discuss the abilities of his associates on the guise if not discussing personalities, is really signaling that he does not want to be measured by his boss.

Badinage

In all organizations a natural group of leaders develops. Participation in membership may be recognized by the spirit of fun, joviality, and needling that the group displays in its daily activities. The organizational chart may show a person to be a member of that group, but even so, he is never a true member of the group if not included in the badinage.

Everyone Has a Boss

He who is not amenable to leadership is not capable of leading.

Leadership

1. Bold, courageous, adaptable
2. Knowledge of job to be done
3. Work: every day, all day, persistent, available
4. Job in gut, not on sleeve

Dwell in the Future

We manage the future, not the past.

The Double Mistake

A good chief executive will do well, if he makes a mistake affecting an associate and the company, to make certain the associate knows that the CEO admits the wrong. Admitted or not, an associate must defend the mistakes of his boss. If admitted, the subordinate can defend in good humor. To cover up doubles the mistake, for the mistakes will be defended with resentment.

Marketing

Salesmen

Good salesmen can sell more mediocre products than poor salesmen can sell good products. And at better prices!

The Marketing Tradeoff

Between quality, price, and service, a company may compete in two but not all three. If quality and service are excellent, price cannot be low. If quality is high and price low, service must suffer.

Marketing Is Selling

Marketing, fundamentally, should be administered under the selling arm of an organization so that it's not impinging tangentially on the sales force. A person can only work for one person; he can't have two masters.

Marketing doesn't pay people, it doesn't promote people, and it doesn't give people a day off to go to the dentist. This is why it is difficult. Marketing must present facts and organization and the results of research to the head of the selling function so that he can implement what is to be done.

Marketing Is a Science

Marketing is the science of what keeps the other fellow awake at night, because when responsible people go to sleep they think about their problems. If you are not solving somebody else's problem, you are not marketing.

The Ballpark

Marketing is having the proper supply of peanuts, roasted, packaged, in the stands, and in the hands of people who can yell, before the end of the first inning. And priced properly to take care of rainy days.

The Good Salesman

How many good salesmen are ruined by becoming sales managers?

Marketing vs. Selling

Marketing is fun; selling is hard work. Most marketing operations are done by people who rub their hands together and say, "What jolly games can we organize today for those guys to carry out?"

Marketing Is a Mud Puddle

All successful companies are run by people who understand marketing, because marketing is by far the most difficult of all the areas of business. You can't kick it, bite it, or scratch it. It's extrasensory. Marketing is like a mud puddle—sort of unclear.

Successful companies know the shape of the mud puddle, how deep it is, where the rocks are. Does it dry up in the spring, replenish in the winter? Who else is playing in the mud puddle? They know the strengths and weaknesses of the competition, and the distribution patterns—jobbers, distributors, direct salesmen, direct mail, retail outlets, representatives. They know the pricing structure, and the mores and customs of the marketplace.

Insurance Salesmen

I have yet to meet the insurance salesman I really like. On examination, this is natural; for an insurance salesman sells a product to a person who doesn't want it, doesn't need it, and can't afford it. Besides all that, it's a terrible investment. Basically, therefore, how could they be nice? All they are interested in is skimming off a commission for themselves.

Distributors

The distributors don't sell a company's products. They enable many people to buy its products. A corollary is: you cannot push your products through the distributors; you may pull them through by demand for the repair parts, or by advertising awareness.

Distribution Agreements

If your company has a distribution agreement to market and sell your product that includes pricing, discounts, etc., you may be in trouble. If you don't control the marketing, you don't control the company.

THE HEARSE

The two most outstanding marketing organizations in the world are the Roman Catholic Church and the life insurance industry. Both drive up in a hearse and then sit on the front porch and talk about the problem. One says, "When you die, if you don't use our service, you will be hot for a long time." And the other says, "If you don't use our service, your wife will hate you forever." The marketing moral is: smart salesmanship implies to the customer if you don't use our product, you'll be in trouble. Crass as it may seem, sales are motivated by fear.

WHO CAN SAY YES

The marketing plan should direct the sales effort to the people in the customer decision-process who can say "yes," and around people who will say "no."

LOSS LEADERS

A loss leader is a great marketing tool, but be certain it leads to a profit.

A Better Mousetrap

Some engineers build a better mousetrap and then try to sell it to people who ain't got mice.

Marketing

All successful companies are run by people who understand marketing.

Salesmen

They should keep their ears open instead of their mouths.

Nationalities

Nationalities

As individuals, we are all the same the world over. None is better or worse than the other because of nationality. But, nations develop an individuality, which covers its citizens as a veneer.

Spanish Could Be a Disaster

Countries with two languages create divisiveness—Quebec, Belgium, etc. Citizens who don't speak the national language cannot participate in the economy and feel rejected. Rejection brings two-way hatred. Please, speak English soon!

Citizens of the World

My country is the world.
My countrymen are all mankind.

—William Lloyd Garrison

Americans

P.T. Barnum once said, "You could never go broke underestimating the intelligence of the American people." But Thomas Jefferson said, "You could never go wrong overestimating the judgment of the American people." How strange that both could be right. Of course, one was a clown and the other a great president.

German Arrogance

For people with the intelligence, skill, culture, and cleanliness of the Germans, the national arrogance reflects a certain rigidity. Rarely will a German listen, and his own sense of logic defeats him. The English knew that the Germans knew that even the English would not be dumb enough to land at Normandy. So, of course, that's where we landed.

Nationality

Even more than religion, nationality is a happenstance of birth. How arrogant to then say, "As an American, I am better than you."

Russian Aristocracy

Under Communism, the artist is an aristocrat. Under capitalism, he is a bum. Shouldn't we think about that?

The Anglo Saxon

His language was earthy and his four letter words enduring. But his sense of human justice and the right of every man to his "castle" created the common law and the foundations of democracy.

An American

If your ancestors stepped off the boat at Plymouth Rock or arrived in Philadelphia or Baltimore in the 1600s, you may consider yourself to be an American. However, the legal immigrant who steps off the plane at Kennedy Airport and says, "I want to be an American" is just as much an American as anyone else. This concept makes our country greater than any other and is what gives hope to all those who wish to come here.

Heritage

Intelligent people are proud of their heritage no matter how humble it may appear to be. Our genes come from many cultures with reflected glory for all.

English Class System

England conquered the world and ruled it for 300 years, but she defeated herself from within by a class system, which prevented the best people from rising to the top.

The Italian Heritage

Of all the nationalities to arrive in this country, it's appalling the lack of credit we give the Italian. For 2,400 years, he has developed organization, music, art, invention, and friendliness. He brought administration to savage Britain before Christ. He produced da Vinci, Michelangelo, Bernoulli, Marconi, Fermi, Columbus, Verrazano, Magellan, and Sophia Loren.

The Nordic Nationality

Finland: The Finns have the national character to withstand Russia and to maintain their integrity. No mean task.

Norway: The Norwegians had the guts to fight the Germans; a one-sided battle, if there ever was one, but they fought on.

Sweden: In two world wars, the Swedes have shown no moral fiber.

Italians

I have never met an Italian I didn't like. A few I didn't admire perhaps! I have never met a Frenchman I really liked. Of course, many to be admired!

Japanese Ratchet Effect

In 1945, as the Japanese signed the surrender on the U.S.S. *Missouri*, someone in Japan decreed, "We lost the shooting war, now begins the undeclared economic war." From that day on, the Japanese sought technology throughout the world, but as a ratchet; it could only flow into Japan, for none is permitted to flow out. This is a brilliant strategy, and the multinational corporations who consistently transfer their technology to Japan are unwitting traitors in an economic war.

The English Language

If you can read, you must be an Anglophile. The English gave us the Magna Carta, Shakespeare, Churchill, and the freedom to work, think, and play.

Guilt

Israel exports guilt to three communities: to the Christians who did nothing in the '30s even though they knew; to the American Jews because they were not there; to the Israeli Jews because they escaped. Eventually, however, no matter who we are, we can only absorb so much guilt.

Military Bureaucracy

Wars are won by the country whose bureaucracy is least inefficient.

The Frenchman's Wife

The Frenchman loves four things more than his wife: his home, his wine, his dog, and his mistress. With such values, how can you build a team?

In World War I, fifty-four French divisions struck and refused to fight, while the English held the line. In World War II, the French lasted six weeks and the British six years. By way of gratitude to the British, de Gaulle came to French Canada and agitated for secession by saying *"Viva le Québec libre!"*

Aerial Bombing Is Also Terror

The Spanish bombed the telephone company on Madrid in 1936. Since that day, bombing has terrified the citizens and magnified their will to resist and worsened their hatred. London, Dresden, and Iwo Jima caused no surrender.

If Reagan's logic to bomb countries that harbor terrorists, such as Libya, is correct, then Thatcher should have bombed South Boston; the Turks, Watertown; and Russia, the JDL in Brookline. (Written in 1987.)

Philosophy

Greed

When greedy men are in financial trouble, they seek help. If that help makes them rich, they are dissatisfied, instantly wanting twice as much and resenting the helper.

Sociologists and Heredity

The sociologist is scared of heredity. The reason is that environment must play a greater part in our ability than heredity, for he can affect environment but heredity is beyond even his control.

"And There Rained a Ghastly Dew"

Enemy foot soldiers respect each other. They see each other in their sights and sight man-to-man. The sailor lays his ship alongside the other and fights what he can see.

The aviator drops his bombs on indiscriminate targets. The people in the fields and cities look up with hatred. The aviator returns a hero to receive adulation from the crowd. In the eyes of God, isn't he a worse criminal than Lieutenant Calley?

THE LIBERAL

The liberal can identify with Angela Davis' civil rights and defend her against a legal system that dares to criticize her for owning two rifles and a shotgun. That liberal mind is so confused that it is totally unconcerned with the civil rights of the judge whose head was blown off by her shotgun. I have yet to meet the liberal who can remember Judge Haley's name. May I also add Frederick Parmenter and his guard, Alessandro Berardelli.

THE TAPES

If you think the only mistake Nixon made was not to burn the tapes, then you should ask some child to help you look up the word "honesty."

Righteousness

Righteousness is that quality that enables a man to burn another at the stake and say, "Thank Thee, Lord, for the privilege of serving."

Congress

Things that look like boondoggles eventually turn out to be so.

Ingratitude

"Blow, blow thou winter wind, thou art not so unkind as man's ingratitude."

—Shakespeare
"As You Like It"

Cheating for the Boss

If an employee, at no matter what level, is cheating, lying, or stealing for the boss, do not ask whether he will cheat, lie, or steal against the boss. The proper question is "when."

BRUTE FORCE

The men in the Navy say it well: "Don't force it, use a larger hammer."

MEMORY OF CONVENIENCE

I never said that!

CROOKED SMILES

The skillful crook smiles sweetly to rebut the accusation. The innocent speak seriously.

WE ASSUME WE UNDERSTAND, BUT...

Complex feedback systems are often counterintuitive.

—*Jay Forrester*

EXAGGERATION

Don't be critical of some exaggeration. After all, if we didn't exaggerate a little bit, no one would ever get married.

—*Eric Hoffer*

NERVOUS ALERTNESS

If the master of the ship is a good seaman, he stands out on the weather side of the bridge. Although uncomfortable, danger comes from that direction. The able seaman develops a sense of nervous alertness, which is one sign of a leader.

VERBS, NOUNS, AND ADJECTIVES

Lincoln's Gettysburg Address was short, succinct, with few adjectives and no long words. His verbs said it: brought forth, conceived, dedicated, created, etc. Harry Truman was an effective communicator because he used verbs and nouns, but few adjectives. The right noun with a verb of action does the job. When a communication is received, if the verbs are underlined, they provide an insight into the writer's real meaning. Instead of giving precision, adjectives diminish the clarity.

Nouveau Riche

We have all heard of second-generation wealth and its evils. Grosse Pointe has too much half-generation wealth.

Judgment

Judgment is that quality which is derived from experience.

Poetry

In life, familiarity breeds contempt. In poetry, familiarity breeds content.

Understanding of a Phenomenon

When: 1 person comprehends, he is a genius.
      3 people comprehend, they are inventors.
      10 people comprehend, they are scientists.
      100 people comprehend, they are physicists.
      1,000 people comprehend, they are technicians.
      100,000 people comprehend, they are students.

The Price of Difference

He who sets himself apart must be willing to be set apart—and eventually set upon.

Double Jeopardy

Bad losers lose twice.

The Paradox of Perspective

When you are 5, a long time is tomorrow.
When you are 10, a long time is a week.
When you are 20, a long time is a year.
When you are 30, a long time is two years.
At 60, a long time is 10 or 20 years.

This may appear to be a paradox, but as the impatience of youth changes to the perspective of age, the mature man plans a longer future. Perhaps we seek a modicum of immortality! And, if we develop a successful plan, it outlives us.

Responsibility

Some people grow with new responsibility, and some people "swell."

Arthur Who?

John Kennedy created two misconceptions. He created the cult of the young and the concept of Camelot. The young have been proven to be arrogant and inexperienced. Camelot never existed; it was always legend.

There Is No Present

There is a past, and there is a future. But, there is no present. For as soon as we say it, it has passed. If we are to influence the future, we must act now, or the future escapes us.

The Impossible

Speak not whereof ye know naught.

Youth

Youth is still too young by definition.

The Horizon

Keep your eyes on the horizon. We cannot run fast or straight, with eyes on the objective, while looking at our feet.

Slow Justice

"The wheels of the gods grind slow, but exceeding fine"—but they never stop turning.

Experience

The one thing you can't learn is experience. But, if smart as well as bright, you will seek advice from experience.

Arrogance

Some men do not overcome arrogance as quickly as they might. If a man is arrogant after the age of 35, he is either covering up dishonesty or is stupid. Nixon,

Agnew, Haldeman, Ehrlichman, Mitchell, and Stans were not stupid.

BRAINS

In life, brains don't count. Judgment does! Bright people without judgment screw up. Dumb people with judgment, win!

PUBLICITY

For all publicity, good or bad, you pay a price.

JOKING

Joking is expressed in one of three fashions. The best is kidding, where the aim is for both sides to have fun. A lower form is teasing, which needles and stings. The worst is ridicule, which is designed to destroy under the guise, "Can't you take a joke?" We kid the people we like; we ridicule those we despise.

HONESTY

Newspapers can't make a story out of honesty.

LIMITATIONS

Sometimes we are more limited by what we know than by what we don't.

LOADED GUN

No one ever seems to be killed with a loaded gun.

GOOD MEN

Good works do not make good men.
Good men do good works.

—Martin Luther

THE WORLD'S MOST IMPORTANT DOCUMENT

At Runnymede, the barons of England wrested from King John protection for the freemen from the caprice of the ruler. On June 15, 1215, John signed the Great Charter of English liberties. Clause 39 provided no freeman could be imprisoned except by the judgment of his peers. What document could be more important in the history of man?

Political Chess

Politicians play the game as though the board contained one king, perhaps a queen, and all of us were pawns. With so many pawns it seems easy to lose a few, but checkmate is bound to come. In the meantime, the bishops, rooks, and knights develop resentment of their pawnship. Will politicians always forget Runnymede?

The Union

When will the American worker understand that if he continues to work at not working, he will lose his job and his living?

Adult Book Stores

A euphemism for porno—it is exactly misnamed. They should be called, "Not Grown-Up-Yet Stores."

Ignorance

Some people don't know what they don't know and are determined to keep it that way. Others know that they don't know and are determined to find out.

Hamlet and Falstaff

If Hamlet is the theater's most important role, then Falstaff is Shakespeare's greatest character. Falstaff epitomizes the weaknesses in men: arrogance, bravado, cowardice, obesity, self-deceit, and belief that they are great lovers.

Great Families

The great families include all generations at their parties. The children are expected to behave and to acquire the mores of the family.

World Domination

1. Rome controlled the world with roads.
2. Britain controlled the world with ships.
3. America controlled the world with planes.
4. Then China with what?

RUTH GORDON

Everyone needs someone to talk to.

—Ruth Gordon
Boston Public Library
October 1982

LINCOLN ROOM

The Lincoln room at the Harvard Club of Boston is decorated with plaques to the presidents, senators, justices, and governors with degrees from Harvard. The inscription reads:

"Dedicated to those selfless men of Harvard who fostered a government of free men."

Harvard taught them to be selfless, which elevated them above the common politician and made them statesmen.

LIFE'S BIGGEST PARADOX

Those who grow up with money know the least about it.

Brilliant Tragedy

Some brilliant people play with the facts instead of working with the facts. By such a small nuance, brilliance becomes dishonesty.

Congress

Why is there a danger that a member of Congress will become either drunk, dishonest, or depraved?

Tragedy

Did Shakespeare believe that tragedy resulted when a strong person became overwhelmed by a serious and fatal flaw in his character? Each of his twelve tragedies appears to be based on one tragic word.

Titus Andronicus	Viciousness
Hamlet	Revenge
King Lear	Ingratitude
Macbeth	Ambition
Othello	Jealousy
Romeo and Juliet	Pride
Antony and Cleopatra	Seduction

Julius Caesar............................... Power
Timon of Athens........................... Hatred
Troilus and Cressida .... War
Coriolanus .... Arrogance

If Pericles, Prince of Tyre, is a tragedy, the tragic word would be lust, but I think it should be classified as a romance.

Conceit

Some people know too much for one person and too little for two.

Ego

Even as leader of their own one-man parade, some men are out of step.

The Game of Life

If you play the game of life so hard you kill your playmates, you will end up with no one to play with.

BRIGHT PEOPLE

One trouble with the very bright is that they overlook the ability of other people to think. They can think in one microsecond; others can think in five and have the answer soon enough.

BUREAUCRATS

Bureaucrats are overbearing in every style of government. They behave as though the citizens were the servants. A subtle distinction exists in a free country.

In a democracy, bureaucrats are confused; they think the people work for them. In a dictatorship, they are not confused; they know the people work for them. We put up with their petty irritation because we could change them if we really had to.

I NEED TO BE SHOCKING!

Modern art, music, dance, prose, speech—all seem to require shock value to be acclaimed by intellectuals. With so much of the world crying for beauty and peace, why should this be so?

Modern generations see themselves as I, we, me, us. To get noticed, they resort to noise and vulgarity. If they stopped thinking of themselves and looked, maybe they could see and hear the beauty.

Back Home

Home is where the wind shifts in the evening, and you can smell the farm down the road.

Political Science

There is no such thing as political science. Science is exact and predictable; politics is an art and cannot be a science.

Political scientists hide behind the mantle of science so they do not have to teach the poisonous art of politics. Students obtain doctorates in political science and yet have learned nothing of the evils of corruption, graft, and not voting. Their doctorates should be in political *arts*.

Giving

He who gives too much, hates the donee, and by him is hated. Do we give because we fear that we are not loved? Do we resent the need to buy this love?

Baby Talk

If you speak with your children as equals, they grow up talking with older people as mature individuals. If you talk baby talk to them, will they ever stop being babies?

Theory vs. Reality

In college the bright student does well, for he is learning theory. In business the slow student may do well, for he is dealing with reality.

Inner City Unemployed

If they can't work, they can't participate. If they don't participate, they hate. We know what hatred leads to.

CONVICTIONS

Sound people have strong convictions. Graceful people prevent their convictions from becoming obsessions.

GUNS

A man doesn't need one to be one.

OVERHEARING

He who eavesdrops deserves what he hears.

JOY

Joy cannot be sought. Joy is a byproduct of hard work.

PEACEMAKERS

We create status for warriors, not peacemakers.

Play vs. Work

The playwright writes a "play," a word which has the connotation of fun and enjoyment. But we speak of his collection as his "works." Curious?

The Game of War

War is the ultimate and only game of men. All other games are lesser copies of war.

Indeed, war may be the final game.

—*Tom Snyder*

Religion

"Faith"

I don't care what a man's religion is, as long as he doesn't believe it.

Old vs. New

The Old Testament	The New Testament
• A God of wrath	• A God of love
• An eye for an eye	• Turn the other cheek
• Ten Commandments all negative (except one, and that's a poor reason)	• Beatitudes all positive
• Heroes—rich men or kings	• Heroes – poor tradesmen
• Story of war	• Hope for peace
• Religion of exclusion	• Religion of inclusion

Both promoted by public relations miracles.

Religious Orthodox

Every religion has its orthodox, and they all pretend to be what they are not. Every religion has some backsliders, and they claim to be what they are.

James and His Bible

King James employed 35 brilliant scholars to translate the Bible in an era of unprecedented English literary skill. Shakespeare may have been one of the first group—all pledged to secrecy. For several hundred years, the English Protestants read daily this beautiful literature.

By serendipity, the English educated themselves in greater numbers than France, Spain, and Italy. This universal learning may have helped to create the democracies that depend on education.

The Diaspora

Although the Diaspora was harsh in the minds of the Jewish people, it may have been what made the Jewish people great. If the Jews had stayed in Israel, a land of sand and stone, would they today have just been a small wandering tribe in the desert?

What could possibly have nurtured a people in that barren land over the past 3,100 years? Scattered to the capitals of the world they both absorbed and contributed culture, science, and education.

Public Schools and Taxes

The public schools are the first line of defense for our democracy. Vouchers or tax money to private schools would build religious schools in which children would learn they were right and the other child was wrong. The concept must be unconstitutional.

The Eleventh Commandment

Moses missed the most important commandment of all: Thou shalt not believe that thy God is better than anybody else's God.

THE MISSED BEATITUDE

When Jesus came down from the mount and delivered His sermon, had He foreseen the modern day Bible-thumping evangelists, He might have added: Blessed are the self-righteous for they shall be called bastards.

VALUE VS. SUCCESS

Through an intermediary, Bishop Fulton J. Sheen asked Einstein what he thought of God. The scientist answered, "I do not know much about God. I am a man of truth. Be not a man of success but a man of value, for a man of success takes more than he gives, but a man of value gives more than he takes."

CATHOLIC COUNTRIES ARE NOT SELF-GOVERNING

Protestant countries are at worst inefficient democracies. Catholic countries are at best dictatorships or revolving republics.

Compare Finland, Sweden, Norway, England, Canada, the United States, New Zealand, and Australia with Mexico, Central America, South America, Spain, and Italy. Only France is in the running, and she is anticlerical.

CHRISTIAN SCIENTISTS

They have been accused of many things, but never charity.

1866

For more than a thousand years many midwives throughout Europe practiced abortion. The Church, in its infinite wisdom, saw no harm for it believed the soul entered the body at the end of the first trimester (three months).

During the American Civil War, with many "camp followers in trouble," the Army doctors discovered "life" at an earlier time. The Churches, both Catholic and Protestant, were embarrassed, and in order to avoid further question, proclaimed the soul enters the body at conception. Suddenly what was right was wrong. If wrong for a thousand years, are we certain we are right now?

Personal Bankruptcy

A man may be bankrupt in several areas:
- Financial
- Moral
- Intellectual
- Spiritual

The spiritual bankrupt is often to be found in church, where in Chapter Eleven, he is trying to work out an arrangement with his principal creditor.

Unitarians

The World Council of Churches frowns on Unitarians because they are not Christian enough. In my experience, Unitarians display more Christian values than the qualifying churches. As individuals, they do Christ's bidding: simple services, help the poor, march in Selma, act with charity, and work for peace.

The China Shop

Late in the Vietnam War, forty-six Quakers met with a general in the Pentagon. They asked him: if two bulls fought in a china shop, whether it mattered who won. His reply is not important. Each of us is a priceless piece of china in the china shop of the world.

A Great President

President Kennedy was one of the greatest presidents we ever had. Nor because of what he did, but because of what he didn't do.

In 1928, Hoover, the Quaker, permitted outrageous statements to be made about Al Smith, the Catholic. During the West Virginia primary in 1960, the Protestants reawakened fear of a Catholic. Joe Kennedy spent one million dollars to be sure that Jack won that primary. Even his brother Bobby had felt Protestant antipathy at Milton Academy. Even so, President Kennedy, even after several drinks, never once said, "Now we'll get those Protestants." He did not submit to Cardinal Spellman, nor did he fuel the religious fires. Thanks to him, the issue is behind us. He deserves everyone's gratitude.

CHARITY AND REWARD

The Quakers believed organized charity was for social climbers. They felt the reward for charity was in their anonymous relationship with God. My wife used to read to several blind people, quietly, in their rooms. One day Theresa, one of the blind students, called and said, "I will *see* you in heaven."

MEN OF GREATEST INFLUENCE

Moses	Law
Jesus	Religion
Marx	Sociology
Freud	Psychology
Einstein	Physics

All were Jews and great thinkers. If we make it for another thousand years, we will know whether they were right.

THE PACIFISTIC QUAKER

Passionately dedicated to pacifism, one-half of the Quakers did not speak to the other half for over 100 years. The dichotomy arose over such a fundamental as the virgin birth. How can people be so embroiled over a totally disputable fact?

The Methodists and Baptists

The Methodists and Baptists represent the heart of the Bible Belt. For several hundred years they read the Bible every day and practiced the worst form of slavery in the history of mankind; while northern fundamentalists prosecuted the Underground Railroad.

The Triumvirate

Albert Cardinal Meyer said at the Second Vatican Council, "It is time we recognize when a country has one religion, then the church, the rich, and the state have everything, and the people have nothing."

Christian Scientists

Every morning the Christian Scientist prays to God for divine guidance. He then believes that whatever he does all day is divinely authorized. Would you believe that group includes Haldeman, Ehrlichman, Krogh, and several other "CREEPs"?

THE CRUCIFIXION

It appears ironic that the Church of Rome for 1,600 years has damned the Jews for the Crucifixion. At the time of Christ, the Jews had no power. Jerusalem was under the control of the Romans who meted out and administered justice. The man in the street may have jeered, but it was the Roman who ordered and executed the task.

RELIGION

Most religions are based on an evil premise: I am right, and you are wrong. Religion has to be dogmatic to support the claim that it is the only true way to salvation. To admit the possibility that another religion has a better route is self-destructive. Since all religion is a happenstance of birth or whom one marries, it's strange that we take it so seriously.

The Mormons

If God really believes that women are equal to men, how can a bigamous religion be as good as one based on monogamy?

Episcopalians

Of the religions I know, I most admire the Episcopalians. They have a beautiful service, a well-educated clergy, they do not proselytize and they could care less whether anybody else belongs.

Ben Franklin and the Quakers

Franklin, the scientist, always the seeker of truth, considered the Quakers to be hypocrites even though their liberal concepts enabled his mind to flourish in Philadelphia when it was not permitted to do so in Boston.

To support Franklin's position, the pacifist Quakers would not raise funds for an army to protect against the French Indians. Finally, the Quakers agreed to give money to buy grain. In their hearts they knew it was for grains of powder. Franklin could not reconcile such hypocrisy.

Birth Control

At the Second Vatican Council, Cardinal Ritter said, "And God said, 'Be fruitful and multiply.'" He said it in a flat world, to two people, in the Garden of Eden. He did not say it in a round world on the plains of Brahmaputra, India.

Water vs. Knowledge

As

Blood is thicker than water,

So

Religion is thicker than knowledge.

Judaism

Man has been around for millions of years. He has had many gods, many of them women. About five thousand years ago the Jews created, out of their own minds, the concept of one God; male, strong, and all-powerful. Then they decided that the God they had created thought of them as the chosen people. Then they decided that the God they had created gave them Canaan forever. So long as these concepts are maintained, the rest of the world will be on the other side of the fence.

WOMEN

WOMEN AND SHAKESPEARE

William Shakespeare was sympathetic to the potential of women!

The Merchant of Venice	Portia had the brains to win the court case and save Antonio.
Macbeth	Lady Macbeth had the nerve to carry out the murder her husband had started.
Much Ado About Nothing	Beatrice was an early version of Jane Austin's Elizabeth Bennett.
Taming of the Shrew	Petrucchino never laid a hand on nagging Kate.
All's Well That Ends Well	He has Diana say, "tis hard bondage to become the wife of a detesting lord."

Cymbeline	Imogen, the king's daughter, is the victim of her husband Posthumus, who wagers on her chastity and then fails to believe in her innocence.
A Winter's Tale	Hermione is falsely accused of adultery. She departs, is presumed dead, and her baby daughter is abandoned on a distant coast.
Othello	Desdemona, a virtuous woman, is murdered by Iago's jealousy.
Antony and Cleopatra	She pretends love but seduces to destroy each of them.

Juliet, Ophelia, Rosalind, Mistress Quickly, Katherine, Volumnia, Cordelia, and many others play strong parts and magnify Shakespeare's belief in the essential role of women in life.

Female Associates

A man in an organization should relate to a woman associate as he does his mother, his sister, or his daughter. To our shame, some men treat women in business as their wives and their mistresses.

Women

What we respect and love we call "she"—our ships, our cities, our countries, our wives and daughters.

Civilization

The level of a civilization may be measured by the dignity and respect with which it treats its women. Not the way its men treat the women, but the way society does as a whole. In addition, the basic unit of a civilization is the family.

Immutable Law of Nature

In nature, there is an immutable law that permits only one female to the nest. In modern society, daughters between the ages of 13 and 20 are still in the nest, and therefore, have conflict with their mothers. As soon as they leave the nest and marry, they regain a closeness to their mothers.

Lust or Love

When little boys want little girls
    They shower affection.
When little boys love little girls
    They shower affection.

She needs to know the difference
Between the body preference
And, to her soul, deference.

Women's Colleges

The Women's Lib movement has successfully wiped out the male college bastion but permitted several of the Seven Sisters to remain exclusively female. Wellesley, Bryn Mawr, Holyoke, and Smith have survived the onslaught. Radcliffe no longer exists. The best women compete to get into Yale, Harvard, and Dartmouth, and questionable men do not have to compete for Vassar and Bennington. One hundred years from now, women will mourn Radcliffe's demise, applaud the Four Sisters who are left, and men will never again regain their colleges.

Use Thy Gumption!

The head of the mathematics department at Swarthmore College from 1870 to 1900 was Susan J. Cunningham. She lived in my grandmother's home and was known as Auntie Cunningham. Had she been a real aunt, it would have been Aunt Susan.

As a woman head of a mathematics department, she was almost a century before her time, but her fame came in urging her students to higher accomplishment with a simple Quaker phrase, "Use Thy Gumption!"

Decency

Tradition tells men to be chivalrous to women; to expect them to have the characteristics of decency, tenderness, kindness, and gentility. In return, over the ages women have nurtured those qualities in all mankind. Now Women's Lib says, not only should women not have those qualities, but men should not treat them as if they do. All mankind will suffer.

A Girl Is What God Made Her

God bestows on Girls
Honesty, love of curls.
But her body beckoning
She is still self-reckoning!

Boys like fair faces
And chase girls with graces,
For they seek full bodies
And try with hot toddies.

The Lady, with mind serene,
Blesses the family scene.
With a fuller sense of Ms.
Her face tells what she is!

The Gentleman, if he be gentle,
Then appreciates her mettle,
And sees that deeper beauty
Built by constant duty.

Fun and Games

Women are fun, but they are not games.

FRIENDS

I have asked several former business associates and clients—now all friends—to comment on their experiences of working with me over the years.

AeroSat Corporation

Michael J. Barrett

Mike Barrett is Founder, Chairman, and CEO of AeroSat Corporation, a leading developer of airborne communications solutions.

As a banker, Art Snyder adds value to companies. He has had a dramatic first-order effect on the company. Dramatic! That's what Art does—in a very quiet, eloquent way.

As we were starting up in 1997, we were turned down by a major New York investment bank because they were interested in just selling the company within a year. This was in the midst of the dot-com craze, and I thought that there had to be someone willing to invest in a company in order to build a business rather than simply trying to make a quick buck.

It was then through my lawyer that I learned that there were only two investors in New England like that, and one was Art. I went down to Boston in my suit and with all of my business plans, and I met Art. I will never forget the meeting.

Art conducts a complete psychological examination of anyone he is looking to invest with. In my case, before our meeting, he learned who I was, what I was, and what motivated me. Then he challenged my views. He opposed whatever view he felt I held strongly in order to measure my communication skills and my ability to respond to something that I vehemently opposed. He told me later that if you are not able to handle that kind of conflict, you cannot run a board meeting. I also learned that he did this all the time to test the caliber of his candidates.

Art has a lot of wisdom. While he is not an expert in any one area of business, he is an expert in identifying people who can take a real leadership role in a new industry and really transform a market. He looked at what we were doing in aerospace from a macro perspective. He told me that the industry has the potential for huge market growth, but also the risk of a very long down cycle. He wanted to know what I was going to do to anticipate that risk and to position the company so we could thrive in both parts of the cycle.

The very next morning, I went on a long business trip that took me to Singapore, London, and Canada. By the time I came home I had synthesized an idea to develop a component technology—based on Art's advice—that is a major opportunity for the company to this day. In fact, right now it's in tests at the FAA.

You won't find an investor better than Art. He likes to say, "I only invest in people. A diversified portfolio is what the ideal investor should be seeking. I seek that through people. I don't seek it through industry concentrations. I don't know what the next new industry is going to be." He takes a contrarian position, and that's why he is so singular and so unique. He's a true gem, and it's hard to find anyone who will speak negatively about him, even if they oppose him. When I asked him, "What kind of people are you looking for?" He said, "They have to have grace." I asked what that meant. He said he can't describe it, but he knows it when he sees it.

I can give you an example of his approach. Early on in the company, I was trying to finish developing our first product. During development the antenna was destroyed. By then I had depleted our revenue. All the investments, all my capital, were gone, and I had no sales yet. I went home and came up with the only plan I could, which was—with a wife and kids at home—to go on unemployment and food stamps for 13 weeks.

I had a couple of hundred thousand dollars on credit cards and I was seeing a lawyer about declaring bankruptcy. After I constructed the plan, I went to see Art. I explained the recovery plan and what had happened. He had many, many questions and was intrigued by my recovery plan. Before the meeting ended, he called up his corporate lawyer and said, "We are extending an advance of $50,000, without condition, to the company. This CEO should not be on food stamps and declaring bankruptcy, because he has what it takes to make the product work." I do not think anyone else on earth would have done that. They would have said, "Okay, let's negotiate," and the terms would have been onerous. He said, "We will negotiate the terms in good faith a bit later." And we did, of course. Since then, the company has done extremely well.

When the chips are down, you know the people who are going to support you. I didn't expect this from anyone, and I left the meeting just shocked—shocked!

Art is still a shareholder, and he is still active with us. He has been offered a large return on his investment that he has declined; he wants to stay with us. When he was our banker he believed it was improper for him to accept personal interest in companies. He is a person of high moral character and he avoids even the appearance of a conflict of interest. When he left the bank in 2005, we asked him to stay on as a board member and we offered him—as we do all board members—stock options. He was able to accept that because the conflict was unwound by that time.

We still ask his advice and counsel. I still come down from New Hampshire to have lunch with him. It's one of these relationships that is very rare; I can ill afford to give it up.

AKIBIA

Thomas Willson

Tom Willson is founder and CEO of Akibia, a leading IT services company based in Westborough, Massachusetts.

Arthur Snyder is as upfront and honest and trusting as you could ever want in anybody. I have learned that a bank can have a powerful position in a company, and you really want them to hang in there when things are tough. You don't want bankers who, as soon as things get tough, decide that they don't want to back you anymore. When I am looking for a banker or an investor, I want someone who is going to be a partner with me. I don't want somebody who I feel I am going to be fighting against. I want straight up, frank communication, and an open and trusting relationship. That is what I get with Arthur.

I met Arthur when Bob Hagopian asked me to join the board of directors of Medica. Arthur was also serving on the board, and when I would see him he would ask me how things were going at Scott Systems, Akibia's predecessor. As time went on and I got to know Arthur, I would be more straightforward with him about what was going on, and at one point I must have been particularly frank about the challenges I was facing. I think Arthur learned to trust me over time, and I learned to trust him as I watched different relationships that he had.

It is very typical in the venture business for the relationship between the CEO and the investor to become adversarial. It can be that way for various reasons; the most obvious one is the business doesn't go well, and the CEO wants to keep going but the investors don't. Art recognizes that we have a business here and that two or three years may not be the optimal for the company to sell. He is willing to look at other alternatives that would allow him to get liquidity in that time frame. Maybe he will leave a little bit of money on the table, maybe he won't get the absolute top dollar, but he allows the company to keep going. He allows me to continue to grow the business if that's what I want to do. And the most important part is that you are very up

Generalizations of a Banker

front and open about it all. It's when you don't have that communication that it becomes extremely difficult, when the investors become impatient to sell. Art's personal qualities of honesty and integrity, and his approach to investing, are favorable to building and growing a company.

Alta Communications

William P. Egan

Bill Egan is a Boston-based venture capitalist and founder of Alta Communications and its predecessor firm Burr, Egan, Deleage & Company. Mr. Egan was previously a partner at TA Associates and manager of venture capital for New England Enterprise Capital Corporation.

I went to the New England Merchants Bank straight out of business school specifically to work with Arthur Snyder because he was really an interesting guy. I went with the understanding that I would get to work with him, and I started out as his gopher.

Someone once asked me, "What was it like working for Art Snyder?" I said, "It was like being an ashtray in a no-smoking restaurant. You were present but useless." He would have somebody come in for a meeting, and I would just sit there. Then I'd clean up after him. At that time, he ran out of his hip pocket the little SBIC called

Generalizations of a Banker

New England Enterprise Capital, which I later took charge of under his command.

Working for him was one of the great lessons in the world because Mr. Snyder (he was always Mr. Snyder to me) would have people come in, and he'd think maybe we should not only make them a loan but also buy a little equity. So he would say to me, "Take a look at this," and I would go back and look. I would think it was totally uninteresting, but I figured if he told me to look at it there must be something interesting there. I soon learned, however, that he would give you this stuff and then it was your problem to figure out whether it was worth wasting your time on it. It really was the greatest training ground for my career in venture capital and private equity because I was getting to look at all these companies that had problems, and I had to determine if they would be successful or not.

He had an uncanny way of evaluating people and situations. First, he is a very smart guy, but he also is a very intuitive guy. It's an interesting combination. He had some unconventional ways of evaluating companies. For example, he never wanted to back someone who was both the president and the treasurer of a business. He'd say that they suffered from "P and T disease"—president and treasurer disease. Fundamentally he was saying, the person who is going to be the CEO or president of the business maybe has to have a very aggressive, positive look at the world. So maybe you want your CFO to be a little more careful, a little more cautious, a little more conservative. It's probably not likely that those attributes are going to be within the same person. Also, he hated the thought of backing a husband and wife team. He would say, "You will never be as close to either of them as they are to each other when they are having pillow talk." He didn't like guys who had beards. It sounds a little quirky, but there was always some underlying rationale for the way he was thinking.

What Snyder intuitively understood was you want to find good businesses, but what you really want to find are great people who can work with those good businesses. During my experience with him, I really learned not only how to evaluate a business, but also how to evaluate people. He backed the guys who started

Generalizations of a Banker

Continental Cablevision in the mid '60s. It's now 40 years later, and I would say to you that those two guys were as good and as capable as any two guys I have met in my entire career in business.

He really believed in backing people who were of high moral character—not that they wouldn't make mistakes, but that they wouldn't lie to you. He paid attention to seemingly little things. If we weren't getting financials in a timely manner then, by definition, it wasn't good news because people always send you good news pretty quickly. In that way, he is a very common-sense kind of person.

One of the things his clients and others who dealt with him didn't totally understand was that he was actually a very good credit guy. He really understood an income statement and a balance sheet. Since he didn't focus on that so much, most people who interacted with him would have said that he is "a people person." They'd say that he was evaluating the people—and he was. But underneath that he also knew whether they were running a good business. If you weren't "inside the tent" with him, you might have thought the only thing he was doing was evaluating the people in your business and how good a person you were. He could have thought someone was a terrific person, but if the business wasn't very interesting, he wouldn't support him.

On the flip side, he might look at a business that wasn't doing as well as it could be, but he would see the growth opportunities. Further, he would understand if these were the people who could drive it. So, he definitely wasn't just a numbers guy, but he really did know the numbers. I think, if anything, that's probably the piece of him that people didn't understand as much. He knew the numbers a lot better than he would let on.

I used to say a lot of times with him that the shortest distance between two points was never a straight line. He would always tack, like in sailing, and he would gain a lot more information from a conversation by moving around a topic rather than addressing it head on. I don't think the business owners could understand how he connected the dots, but if you worked with him you could. He had a way of making entrepreneurs comfortable by having a conversation where he would say, "I don't quite get this," when in fact he got it very well. Because he had been the technology lender on Route 128 to smaller companies, people would be a little on guard when they came to see him. Then he would get talking with them, and he'd make them feel very at ease. It was his way of drawing them out in order to understand their reality. He would have made a phenomenal business school professor with his way of not giving answers, but by just asking questions.

    I tell people that I only had two jobs before I started Burr, Egan, Deleage in 1979. I worked for Arthur Snyder at the New England Merchants and then I worked for Peter Brooke at TA. There is absolutely no question those two people defined my career. I feel tremendous gratitude to both of them.

ATWOOD & MORRILL

Byron T. Atwood, Jr.

Byron Atwood is the former president of Atwood & Morrill, a manufacturer of engineered valves, founded in 1900.

Art was unique among bankers. He had the talent, the desire, and the vision to understand and articulate what actions a business needed to undertake to succeed. He had the foresight to visualize what could be, and he could realistically view what was. He took great personal satisfaction in a client's success.

I was in my early thirties and inexperienced. I had just become CEO of a family-owned valve company that was in financial trouble. Financial management was poor, but the company's product and reputation were excellent, which Art confirmed through his own investigation. Three banks had refused to lend us additional necessary money, but Art did. He probably was the only banker in New England who would. Subsequently, the business prospered. His help, counsel, and encouragement were a vital part of the company's success.

Concordia Company, Inc.

Robert A. (Brodie) MacGregor

Brodie MacGregor, raised on the west coast of Scotland, is President of Concordia, a full-service boatyard located in South Dartmouth, Massachusetts.

My first banking contact with Arthur Snyder was unusual, but not, I suspect, atypical.

I was working in a New England boatyard, which some years prior had built Arthur's schooner Welcome. One cold spring Saturday morning, I looked out of my office window and observed Arthur high up in Welcome's rigging. Later, I walked down the wharf and Arthur was still up there on the foremast. It seemed to me that he was struggling a little and I asked if I might help in any way. "What the hell do you know?" came back the response.

After a while, Arthur came down to warm up in front of the cabin stove, surrounded by glowing butternut joiner work. He asked me a lot of questions about myself, what I had done, and what I hoped to do in the future. I explained that I was hoping to buy the yard, but I didn't know how to finance the purchase.

Arthur explained that the computers at Commonwealth Bank and Trust might not react favorably to my numbers, but he didn't seem to care. He continued to ask about me, what I thought about various aspects of the company, and what changes I would plan to make.

Early the next week I was at the bank. The loan officer asked some appropriate questions, and Arthur continued to talk about the future of the boatyard. Later, Arthur fixed his eyes on me and said that they didn't always pay attention to the computer, but they always paid attention to his gut feeling. He told me he wanted me never to forget that if he loaned the money, he expected to get it back.

Well, Arthur did make the loan and we did pay it back, but more importantly I've been fortunate enough to consider Arthur Snyder one of my close friends for nearly 30 years.

Continental Cablevision

Amos Hostetter

Amos Hostetter is Chairman of Pilot House Associate, LLC, and was the Co-founder, former Chairman and Chief Executive Officer of Continental Cablevision, Inc.

Arthur Snyder is one of a kind, and he is the living definition of an iconoclast.

Continental Cablevision never would have happened without Arthur. He made an outrageously risky term loan to us in 1963 when nobody was making term loans to cable companies, and very few people even knew what cable companies were all about. When we sold the company in 1996—33 years later—we had over 10,000 employees. These were all jobs that Arthur created.

Before he financed Continental Cablevision, I had a banking relationship with Arthur. One of my closest friends was a graduate student at MIT who was doing his Ph.D. thesis on econometric modeling of commodity prices. There had been a frost in Florida, and he called to tell me that the market hadn't reacted to what was clearly going to be a damaged citrus crop. "We should buy concentrated orange juice," he told me.

"What are we going to do with it?" I asked.

"We are just going to keep it," he said.

So we went to Arthur and convinced him that he ought to loan us $10,000 to buy concentrated orange juice. It stayed in a food warehouse, and we never took delivery of it. Nine months later, we sold it back to the same wholesaler, Quincy Cold Storage, for twice our investment.

Then, in the spring of 1963, Irv Grosbeck and I were granted the cable franchises in two towns in northwestern Ohio. I was living in Marblehead for the summer, and Arthur lived in Marblehead as well. We both worked on State Street in Boston at the time, so we carpooled together. Over the course of the summer, he would ask me how the cable deal was going. At the end of the summer he told me, "Here is what I am going to do for you. I want you to talk to everyone else who might be a potential lender to this. At the end of that, come tell me what you've got, and we'll see if I can do better."

By December of that year I had been to every bank in New York, Chicago, and Philadelphia that might have some knowledge of cable television. In every case we got the same answer: "It sounds like a great idea. After you get it up and running and you have some positive cash flow, come see us, and we'll talk about lending you some money." Well, obviously the project would never have started if we needed to have positive cash flow as a condition of financing.

So I went to Arthur, and he spared me the embarrassment of asking what the next best offer was, because there wasn't one. I brought him this loose-leaf notebook, which was the prospectus for the company. In it we had the ambitious goal of having, some day, as many as 25,000 customers. (When we sold the company, we had 4 million, so it exceeded our expectations by just a bit.) Arthur took the notebook from me, and he ceremoniously walked over and dropped it in the wastepaper basket and said, "Now tell me about your company."

He didn't want to see anything in writing; it was all face-to-face and eye-to-eye. He then laid out the provisions for a potential term loan. We need $600,000, and he said, "I will loan you half the money, if you get $300,000 in equity first."

"Will you give me a letter to that effect?" I asked.

"Yes, I will."

Based on the strength of that letter, we were able to raise the equity, and the company got started.

The interesting footnote to this story is that three or four years later, during a meeting to refinance the loan, he said, "There's one thing I forgot to tell you when I described the terms of your initial loan."

"What's that?" I asked.

"Well, you are going to sell the bank five percent of the company at the original price."

"Yes, you did forget to tell me that," I said, "And yes, I will."

My relationship with him and my trust in him were such that I said, "Of course, you've earned it." Eventually, we bought back the stock at 40 times what the bank had paid for it—a huge markup.

Generalizations of a Banker

It's an old saw in the banking business that people pay back loans, balance sheets don't. That was the basis on which he operated. I think he made an assessment over the course of the summer of '63, that Irv and I were guys he was willing to bet on.

The source of Arthur's success is that he is a great judge of character. He had a famous set of "rules" on which he based his judgments, though I think they were all after-the-fact creations. That is, I think he basically made judgments about people and then tried to construct a framework describing what had been successful. Ultimately, I think it was just his gut instinct.

I think he was making a statement by dropping our prospectus in the wastebasket. I don't think he ever put much weight on financials. I am not sure how well he reads financial statements, because in my experience, I never saw him look at one. He would look you in the eye and ask, "Tell me, why do you think that's going to work?" and "What are you going to do next?" Then he would get off on some totally unrelated subject that I subsequently came to understand was his way of probing your thinking on a range of subjects. He would bait you and see what your tolerance was for outrageous assertions.

They did a case at the Harvard Business School on Continental Cablevision, and he used to love to go there and say, "Now, let me tell you about this term loan I made in 1963. I made a $300,000 loan, the company prospered, grew, and five years later paid it down to 10 million." Anything just to be provocative! His point, though, was you don't expect to get loans paid off by successful companies. It's quite the reverse; you know that the amount of borrowing is only going to go up.

There is a group of companies in New England that wouldn't have happened without Arthur Fenimore French Snyder. He was a real positive force in the community. I'm a great fan of Arthur's; he has a very special place in my heart.

DORIS KEARNS GOODWIN

Doris Kearns Goodwin is a Pulitzer Prize winning author and historian, an NBC News analyst, a former assistant to President Lyndon Johnson, and a lifelong baseball fan.

In the mid-1980s, I was working on *The Fitzgeralds and The Kennedys*, a book that eventually took me ten years to write. I was finishing the book at the Boston Athenaeum, working on the top floor of that beautiful five-story neoclassical building across from the State House on Beacon Hill. The reading room is surrounded by balconies of books—it's a glorious place to write. My husband and I were living on Beacon Hill just for a year, so I was working there rather than in our house.

It is often the case that a publisher's advance doesn't last until the book is done, so there was a period of time when I was still writing without a regular salary coming in. It was during that period that Arthur lent us some money. Once the book was published, we were able to pay back the loan.

It seemed to me that the most important criteria he looked for in deciding who to loan to was the character of the person. That was more important, in many ways, than the balance sheet or the amount of collateral they could put forth. He liked to get a sense of who the person was. In turn, I got a sense of him, and we became friends.

Arthur's office was near the Athenaeum, so he would just stop by sometimes to say hello, ask how I was doing, and we'd talk for a little while. He would ask about my writing, how I got into it, and why I liked doing what I was doing. By showing interest in my writing, he got a sense of the passion that I had for my work. Those conversations probably told him a great deal about our ability to use the loan wisely and pay it back in a timely fashion, because he trusted that I loved the work I was doing. He obviously loved what he was doing, so I think he understood that if you really had a passion for what you were doing, it was also more likely everything was going to work out well.

I felt like he was part of my project, not simply some anonymous banker who loaned us money. We felt somehow responsible to him, to make sure everything came out right. We also developed a good relationship, and there was that sense of connection between us. At times, he invited us to go sailing with him on that incredible boat of his, and we got to know his wife, Jean, as well.

I felt that he was like the neighborhood banker in the old days who was a central figure in the community. My father was a bank examiner on Long Island, so I knew that world of banking when I was a little girl. That world changed with the advent of large banks that focused on mergers and acquisitions. In these transactions, you might not even know who your banker is. In some ways, Art Snyder reminded me of what it was like in those earlier days. He really saw the role of a banker as one who helps people.

Jamesbury Corporation

Howard G. Freeman

Howard Freeman served for thirty years as Chairman and CEO of the Jamesbury Corporation, a leading manufacturer of valves, based in Worcester, Massachusetts.

I met Art Snyder at a social gathering around 1950, and in those years people were always free to talk about their wartime experiences. As we shared ours, we realized we shared a most unusual coincidence. In September 1942, Art was a junior officer on the troopship USS Wakefield, which was a converted ocean liner, the SS Manhattan. Somewhere off Nova Scotia, the ship caught fire; it was a very difficult and unhappy situation. Some destroyers came to help put out the fires using some very new nozzles that were unusually and remarkably effective. Their efforts saved the ship and everybody on it, including Art Snyder. I am the inventor of those nozzles. And that's the reason why Art and I got to be so friendly.

Generalizations of a Banker

In 1954, I started the Jamesbury Corporation to make valves. I got hold of Art Snyder and sought his help with our banking needs. He also gave us valuable advice. Soon he became a director of the corporation and stayed in that position for almost 30 years. Eventually, we had more business than we could manage, and he was very helpful in funding the cost of manufacturing until we could get paid by our customers. The company was sold in 1984 to Combustion Engineering. At the time we had 3,000 shareholders, subsidiaries around the world, and about 2,000 employees.

When it came to personal integrity, honesty, and truthfulness, he had them in spades! Early on at the company, we brought in Arthur Andersen to do our accounting, and they remained our accountants throughout the 30 years. At that time, Arthur Andersen was really two companies; they had the accounting company and a consulting company. Art was adamant. He said, "You can't have both accounting and consulting from the same company. There is a conflict of interest." With the disappointment of Arthur

Andersen, we chose not use their consulting group because we realized that the quality of that consulting would be compromised. And, of course, decades later that arrangement blew up like mad with the Enron scandal, and it caused the demise of Arthur Andersen.

Art was also quite outspoken, though he was not always right. I had a young engineer working for me who emigrated from Portugal, put himself through engineering school at Worcester Polytechnic Institute, and then got an MBA at Clark University. He was so bright, and he wanted to go into accounting. At one point we had an opening, and Joe came into my office and said, "Howard, I want that job!" I wanted to give him the job, but Art, alone among all the directors, objected. Well, you see, Joe had a mustache, and Art didn't believe in people who wore mustaches. After some training and mentoring, Joe got the job, and he worked out extremely well. Art was absolutely gracious about it, and eventually, he and Joe became very good friends.

He operated on principles; one is that he is straight with people. That's my personality, too. We had one director, a prominent and successful businessman, who didn't like Art. He came to me and said, "It's either Art or me." And I said, "Well, it was good knowing you."

MEDICA CORPORATION

Robert W. Hagopian

Bob Hagopian is CEO of Medica, a leading manufacturer of blood testing analyzers based in Bedford, Massachusetts.

When Medica was first started in 1983, we needed venture capital funding. Arthur Snyder was well known as the person to go to.

My first meeting with Arthur was jovial, but it was also the first time he threw me a curve ball. You see, Arthur has a funny way about him. When he wants to test people, he tells them the exact opposite of what he's thinking, to see if they agree with him. I don't recall the exact question, but Arthur wanted to determine whether the founders, who were asking for more stock options, were really interested in attracting and keeping good employees or whether we were all being greedy. I wasn't quite sure what to make of that first meeting, but he eventually agreed to put some seed money into

Medica. Then he became a director, and the business finally got off the ground.

Arthur's role as a director hasn't changed very much in all these years. He listens, gives advice, and is constantly testing people. That's the way he operates. He is not interested in the numbers. His habit of saying the opposite of what he really thinks is just one in his bag of tricks.

At one meeting, there was a split in the board and Arthur voted with the management instead of with the other venture capitalists, which caused an unbelievable commotion. The venture capitalists were very upset. They took it personally. A few months later, Arthur, in Quaker tradition, went down to Connecticut to make up with them, though I don't know how much "making up" there was. Arthur makes his decisions based on facts, and he votes his own way; he's very independent in that regard. He is still a director today and comes to the meetings. Sometimes, when you think he's asleep, he's not. Rather, he is listening to absolutely everything.

He has been a good mentor to me. I remember one time I had to decide which of two employees to lay off, since we didn't have enough money to pay both of them. Art gave me good advice. He wanted me to keep the guy who had values similar to his. He felt that this person was a good manager of people, while the other was just a technocrat. He simply said, "You can replace technocrats, you can't replace good management people." I followed his advice, and it was one of the best of decisions I made at Medica in twenty years.

He loves to talk about religion, politics, and people's national origin. When I call him, I just leave a message, "This is the Armenian, give me a call." He knows who it is. He is all for making provocative statements, but you never know what's behind them. Sometimes he deliberately tests people, but at other times he's simply being facetious. People who meet him for the first time don't know what to make of him. Arthur is an enigma.

SOFTRAX

Robert O'Connor

Bob O'Connor is President and CEO of Softrax, a leading provider of revenue management software, based in Canton, Massachusetts.

Softrax Corporation would not be in business today if it were not for Art Snyder. Art provided our first outside investment of $400,000 that allowed us to achieve our subsequent levels of growth. Since then, we have grown substantially more; we attracted over $20 million in additional investment, grown our customer base to hundreds of companies across the globe, and have achieved a reputation as an industry leader in revenue management software. As usual, Art was ahead of his time in seeing our potential.

While he has many great attributes, Art's judgment of people stands above all others. After a brief conversation, Art could tell you more about a person after just a few moments than others would be able to ascertain in days or even months. He could tell whether someone is a "good person" or not. He could immediately tell whether someone was honest, trustworthy, and committed to the business. He was never wrong. I wish I could say the same for myself.

While serving on our board of directors, Art was able to grasp and communicate the essence of our most challenging issues. He kept us focused on the critical issues, and coached me to do the same. He has played an invaluable role in starting Softrax and as a personal friend. I am eternally grateful for both.

Ted Hood Yachts

Frederick E. (Ted) Hood

Ted Hood is a world-renowned yachtsman, sail maker, and boat builder. As skipper of the 12-meter yacht Courageous, he won the America's Cup in 1974.

Art Snyder is different than all the other bankers I have known; he has common sense. I probably wouldn't have survived without him.

At some point I was building about four or five boats overseas and I was issuing letters of credit. So, I went to meet with a group of eight bankers to get some loans and a line of credit. We were sitting around a table discussing the loans I wanted, and after about an hour I got sick of it and said, "Excuse me, gentlemen" and walked out to call Art. I told him about the situation and what I needed to do. He said, "Don't worry about it, I'll take care of you." Boom! Just like that. So I went back in the room and said, "Sorry gentlemen, I am going somewhere else."

I guess he had faith in me because of my sail business and the other things I had done. We knew each other because I built a thirty-seven-foot sailboat for him thirty or more years ago and I probably made sails for some of his boats, too. Art's a great sailor. He raced with me a lot, good long-distance races. Not only is he a great sailor, he's a real bright guy, really bright about a lot of things.

He's just a practical, hands-on, seat-of-the-pants type of guy, and his approach to banking was more personalized. He sized up the people running the business and decided whether or not they were going to make it. The kind of people they were and ideas they had were more important than just going by the numbers.

THE YANKEE GROUP

Howard M. Anderson

Howard Anderson is Founder and former President of The Yankee Group, co-founder of the Boston-area venture capital firms Battery Ventures and YankeeTek Ventures, and the William Porter Distinguished Lecturer at MIT.

When I started my career in Boston in the late '60s, I was a young guy working for a high-tech company in East Cambridge, and Arthur was the man to see if you were in high-tech. When you went to visit Arthur at New England Merchants Bank, he would ask you a series of questions to which he already knew the answer. He wanted to see if you knew the answer. He would ask, for example, "What's your sales?" If you were a CEO and you didn't know the number, he would be not happy. He would tell a CEO, "Your financial guy has to run the right side of the balance sheet, and you have to run the left side."

When he was looking at a business, he was evaluating two things. First, he looked at your idea and determined if there was a need for it. At the same time, he would look at you and your team. Then, if he liked both the idea and the people, he thought you would probably succeed. If he liked you but not your business idea, he would give you advice, but not money.

He was doing venture capital before there was venture capital; so he was essentially making risky loans based often on his gut feeling of these people. Arthur was there at the creation. Guys like George Dorio get a lot of credit in town for doing venture capital, but there was a need for ongoing capital after guys like Dorio got a company started, and Arthur was providing debt capital.

He was the most charismatic banker in town. His advice was solid, he worked hard, he knew everybody, and he was energetic as hell. His contact list was without peer. He knew everybody in town, and if you thought that you had a product that Raytheon could use, he would whip out his Rolodex while you were there, make a call, and you got an appointment with the guy at Raytheon. He had a phenomenal memory, and he built a good staff inside New England Merchants Bank.

He also had this set of Warren Buffett style rules; if you followed them, you did well and people listened. For example, he wanted the CEO to go see two customers a day. Plus, you needed to make sure that no single customer is too much of your business, because if they go out of business, you'll go out of business. There are probably eight or ten of those guidelines. They weren't brilliant insights, but good lessons to learn that addressed the fundamentals of running a business.

One of his lessons to me was: get profitable as soon as you can because you have a lot better options, and you will sleep a lot better. So that's what I did. He also warned me against taking some other people's money, so I took no one else's money, and did it without any venture capital. I teach now at MIT, so I am teaching Arthur's lessons to the next generation.

Throughout his career, Arthur dispensed money and advice, and the advice was probably more valuable than the money.

Metamorphoses

Over the course of my life, I have awakened to new views on various topics. What follows are explanations of how those transformations came about.

POLITICS

I was a Republican all my life until Nixon, who changed my politics completely. I am still a registered Republican, but I would not vote for one. They seem to be on the wrong side of every issue. Now I support the Democrats. Please don't tell my uncle, who has been dead since 1960. He'd stand up in the grave and have me shot. He was a Quaker, but not a good one.

RACE

My twin brother Paul and I had a good relationship with blacks during our childhood and upbringing. A black man, Lee Talliaferro (which was pronounced Toliver), drove us to school and worked for the family. During World War II, I had a Navy mess attendant named Ransom who brought me coffee and shined my shoes every morning. The mess attendants could not "strike" for any rate higher than Steward's Mate. Then

Eleanor Roosevelt said to Franklin, "I know the games you're playing, so do me a favor and get the Navy to allow blacks to strike for anything they want." Ransom became a Machinist's Mate. I was the Chief Engineering Officer, and he worked in my department and did an amazingly good job. I learned that all the blacks needed was the opportunity. They were totally capable, as has been proven.

RELIGION

My mother was a Quaker. My birth certificate says, "Religion: Quaker." However, my grandmother, whose husband had died of tuberculosis, switched to Christian Science and brought along her daughters, which included my mother, so I grew up in the Christian Science religion. Fortunately, I was not really a believer. I learned to be a Quaker at the schools I attended (Media Friends School, Haverford School, and Swarthmore College) and at home. In our home, we followed the Quaker tradition and spoke to each other in the familiar tongue. We spoke to each other with the words "thee" and "thy."

When my son Tom was twelve years old I was afraid that he had polio so I called in a doctor and he said, "No. It's just growing pains." So, I said to myself, "If it had been polio, who would be responsible if I had followed the concepts of Christian Science and did nothing about it?"

In my opinion, there are illegal and immoral aspects of Christian Science. My wife and I decided to visit the Episcopal Church and the Unitarian Church. Both made good sense to us, so we started to attend. She eventually became a Unitarian but I rejoined the Friends Meeting—Beacon Hill Friends. I can't brag about my membership, for I don't attend very often, but I do support it financially at a modest level.

WOMEN

In the banking system I hired ten to twelve trainees from the business schools every year. In the late 1960s, I hired a woman from the Harvard Business School. The bank's personnel officer criticized my waste of an employment opportunity, so I dug into what he was paying the other trainees and found she was paid a thousand dollars a year less than the men. I immediately sent her a telegram improving her salary. The personnel officer screamed, but I didn't have to listen. Barbara Draper turned out to be an outstanding officer. She is now president of a bank. This led me to realize the enormous potential of women in the work force, and I continued to support them whenever and wherever I could. They were an untapped resource.

Welcome

A topsail schooner built by Concordia in 1984, and rigged by Arthur Snyder. Circumnavigated the North Atlantic Ocean, 1985.

www.ingramcontent.com/pod-product-compliance
Lightning Source LLC
Chambersburg PA
CBHW071423170526
45165CB00001B/377